How to Be a
Stress Free, Worry Free
Woman

by

DR. GILDA CARLE

Published in New York by
InterChange Communications Training, Inc.

Copyright © 2016 InterChange Communications Training, Inc.

Gilda-Gram® is a registered trademark owned by InterChange Communications Training, Inc.

Disclaimer: Private individuals depicted throughout this book are composites. To protect privacy interests, all names and identifying details have been changed, and emails have been adapted or paraphrased.

All rights reserved under international and Pan-American Copyright Conventions. No part of this publication may be reproduced, stored in a retrieval system or transmitted, in any form or by any means, electronic, mechanical, photocopying, recording or otherwise, without the prior permission of the copyright holder.

ISBN-13: 978-1-881829-09-6

Library of Congress Control Number: 2015904245

Printed in the United States

For more information visit
www.DrGilda.com

ACKNOWLEDGMENTS

Thank you to all who have so generously contributed your true stories to help others who are reading this book. Without your giving, there would be less healthful living!
--Dr. Gilda

<u>Gilda-Gram®</u>
**Busting your stress from worry
is the ONLY way
to reach emotional and physical health.**

CONTENTS

INTRODUCTION
Everyone Worries   i

CATEGORY I.
Stress in Love Relationships
    Worry #1. Finding Love   1
    Worry #2. Keeping Love   7
    Worry #3. Losing Love   11

CATEGORY II.
Stress in Other Relationships
    Worry #4. Friendships   15
    Worry #5. Children   19
    Worry #6. Parents   24

CATEGORY III.
Stress in Health, Looks, & Finances
    Worry #7. Physical Health   29
    Worry #8. Finances   37
    Worry #9. Feeling Attractive   51
    Worry #10. Being Alone   60

CONCLUSION
Take This Dare   62

INTRODUCTION

Everyone Worries

Yes, everybody worries, although some people hide it better than others. From my Advice and Coaching internationally online from my website, **www.DrGilda.com**, and from my other clients, readers, and fans, I have found that the Number One stumbling block in life for both men and women is worry. Yet, ironically, all the chaos we create inside ourselves usually turns out to be needless in the end, as most of these feared catastrophes never come to pass.

Different cultures offer their own special remedies for dealing with anxiety and stress, from worry dolls, to worry beads, to Ben Wa Balls, to worry stones, and so much more. In our own culture, women worry more than men—sometimes twice as much—and, according to the American Psychological Association's Task Force Report on Women and Depression, women become more depressed over our worries. It's especially interesting that the discrepancy between the sexes on a fictitious "Worry Meter" is due to this very interesting fact:

Gilda-Gram®
Men don't *need* to worry so much, because their women take on that burden for them!

In a survey of 1,487 men and women at the University of Michigan's Institute for Social Research, it was found that women ages 35 to 49 worry most about "people oriented" issues, and they allow these problems to constantly nag at them. Unlike men, most women suffer multiple life demands in their work and family life that feed them guilt about not measuring up to being a "superwoman." And this then becomes a true paradox: They feel guilt if they *don't* measure up, but they're burned out if they *do*.

The top worries for the surveyed women included living costs, unexpected expenses, social problems, household tasks, children, time for self, environmental issues, partner/spouse problems, employer issues, and physical appearance. The Lahey Clinic's Department of Psychiatry and Behavioral Medicine suggested women's major worries center around time, relationships, and physical appearance. Considering these findings, I grouped women's worry categories into three distinct categories: Love Relationships, Other Relationships, and Well-Being.

Since men have women doing much of their worry work, they've trained themselves to get off the hook by becoming distracted with activities that offer an escape from their everyday stressors. Most women can attest that when their guy is faced with a crisis, he knows how to drop out. Instead of obsessing over an issue the way a woman would, men are better at becoming immersed in work, or in a favorite sport or TV program, or they hang out with friends, or they simply go to sleep. Harboring their worries, rather than safely channeling them, is not the healthiest thing a man can do, but it does limit their vulnerability to perceived pain.

Diane is a Ph.D. married to Marc, an M.D. When their two children were small, Diane was always nervous to let Marc take them to the park to play. She said he let them do dangerous things on the playground equipment, and they often returned home with bruises. In contrast, when Diane took the kids to the park, she watched them like a hawk, and was far stricter than Marc in what equipment she allowed them to sample.

When women worry, we allow our problem to engulf our entire life, as we analyze it from every angle with our closest friends, and thus we permit it to overwhelm us. Yet, if there was one positive effect about the way women worry, it would be that by sharing our concerns, we do let them out of our body. On the most positive side, if we can spill our guts to a loved mate who will listen and offer feedback, there's a life-saving payoff: Researchers at the University of North Carolina found that spouses who receive emotional support from their mates are at lower cardiovascular risk than those who don't.

In our culture, men and women fall into their

worry roles as soon as they bond. As little girls, many women watched their mothers worry as they waited at home while their fathers toiled at work. Even children of working mothers grew up seeing their moms as the worry warrior for their home and family.

Consequently, today's adult women mirror the behaviors they observed in childhood. They accept the draining role of designated worrier as a means of feeling they are actively involved and in control of otherwise uncontrollable events. But little do they know about the "seesaw effect" that they unwittingly take on:

Gilda-Gram®:
If one mate worries, the other doesn't have to.

Worriers are typically people who feel they lack control, and are therefore vulnerable to others. They misguidedly believe that by worrying, they can actively direct what happens next. But when the worry gets out of hand, misinformation and exaggeration lead their emotions. Clarity of thought ceases, and effective solutions are blocked. Instead of being in the here and now, the person is in the regrettable place of there and then, or even the more confusing, where and when. She then expands her worrying even further, and builds even less hope for change.

Obsessive worry is a waste of time and effort because it debilitates you. It impacts your work, your life, and your health. The people who worry aimlessly are called "obsessive worriers." Most obsessive worriers remain stuck in worry mode, writing imaginary scripts that can even evolve into lengthy novels. Fortunately, these story lines exist only between the worrier's ears, and rarely come to pass. However, the worrier often does plenty of damage to her relationships and her body by the time she figures that out.

Besides consuming someone so much that they distract her from fulfilling the goals that will enhance her life, depression, anxiety, panic attacks, a compromised autoimmune system that invites illness, drug and alcohol addiction, and fractured relationships are dangerous outgrowths of excessive worry. Moreover, excessive worry elevates blood pressure and increases the risk of heart attack.

On the other hand, all is not bleak. Worry can be productive—if a person uses it to alert her about upcoming danger that demands attention. "Productive worriers," as they're called, gather facts, dig for deeper meaning, find appropriate solutions, and take action. Thus, most successful people know how to worry "effectively," by following this healthful credo:

<u>Gilda-Gram®</u>
Let your worry PROPEL you,
not PARALYZE you.

Therefore, by taking action, a person will put

herself in charge of her circumstances—and thereby turn the tide on the event that caused a worry domino effect. Productive worriers make worry work for them, differentiating between the things they can control, and those they can't.

Of course, no one can control another person—so productive worriers give up that one up as a possibility. But this way, they can give up that notion and concentrate on the events that are changeable, and which require the use of sure-fire methods to silence the demons. Productive worriers therefore find and apply solutions that become the conduit that takes them further and higher, to greater success in every aspect of their lives.

CATEGORY I.
Stress in Love Relationships

Worry #1:
Finding Love

From the moment little girls discover little boys, they fantasize that when they are older, they will meet a special "prince" who will sweep them off their feet and take them to his castle to provide the promise of "happily ever after." Even if a mother has not breast-fed her daughter with this brand of mythology, somehow her little darling still dreams of Prince Charming saving her from her own, less-than-happy life.

Magda was a conscientious, stay-at-home mom. She often described herself as "Mother of the Millennium," a woman who was hip in teaching her two daughters to become self-sufficient and independent, whether or not they had a man. In support of her beliefs, she was dutifully saving money for each of her girl's college educations, so they would become educationally savvy, and financially sound on their own.

When her older daughter joined the girl scouts, Magda became a scout leader, happily accompanying the troop on their occasional outings. It was when she took her tiny four-year-old along with her on one of these park trips that she suddenly got a rude awakening. Standing under a shady tree, she found little Prissy stroking a dirty, warty frog. A devout observer of cleanliness, Magda screamed, "Priscilla, put down that awful creature." But Prissy stood her ground. She staunchly shouted back, "No, mom, I'm gonna kiss this frog so he'll turn into a handsome prince." With that, the little child planted a juicy, wet kiss on the filthy amphibian.

Flabbergasted, Magda wondered, "Where did she get the frogs-become-princes notion? Certainly, not from me!" But at that moment, Magda had to accept that as much as a fastidious mom tries to keep the fairy tales out of her home, the belief that the prince is on his way still prevails. Perhaps this story line is transmitted through school friends, the media, books, and the general culture. But whatever the source, most little girls grow up believing that if a prince is not in hot pursuit, there's something wrong with them!! And they worry about this at an earlier and earlier age.

Dear Dr. Gilda,

I've wanted a boyfriend for a long time. Now I'm 12 years old. Is love at first sight possible? I met this incredible guy, and I think I love him, although it's only been one week.
Jennifer

HOW TO BE A STRESS FREE, WORRY FREE WOMAN

Dear Dr. Gilda,
I am a 13-year-old girl and I have a boyfriend for the first time, and well, he is experienced in the kissing department, but I'm not. I need help on the tongue thing, and when, how, and what to do, because I don't want him to go to another girl who knows more than me.
Heidi

Sure, science documents that today's girls are menstruating at earlier ages than they ever have. Along with their body's maturity comes an awareness of the opposite sex, and a boy-craziness around which their entire world revolves. Young girls are miserable if they don't have a boyfriend. During their teen years, they go through "relationships" as quickly as they change their underwear. If they feel they lack success in getting someone to "love" them, they question their self-worth—and I get many, many tearful emails. Some girls actually leave for college thinking they're social failures, because they haven't yet found love. And when these girls graduate four years later, despite the fact that they're actively pursuing important careers, many still feel that their first priority is to find the proverbial "prince."

TV is ripe with examples of what a girl will do for love. Years ago, in television history, the character Felicity in the show by the same name, chose to go to a college of lesser status to follow her crush, rather than go to the prestigious one to which she had been accepted. An even older version on the same theme,

Ally McBeal portrayed a noteworthy attorney, but despite her fine professional credentials, she believed her life was worth nothing without a man, and she was not ashamed to whine about it. These were two very popular shows at one time, whose popularity hinged on the identification their audiences felt with the characters. Both characters loudly worried and complained about not having a guy, and this concern pervaded their lives and career choices.

The problem with worrying about finding love is that it engenders fear, which clouds vision, and propels us to make poor choices. Women who are compulsive about finding love become less discriminating about selecting an *appropriate* partner.

In desperation, too many women wind up settling for someone who is less worthy of them, whom they don't respect, or who doesn't respect them. At first, the objective for many was just to have a warm male body to sleep next to, which would signal to the world that these women are loved. But selecting the wrong partner could mean unhappiness in the years that follow the honeymoon, a couple of children later, as a woman questions how she ever ended up in such a miserable predicament.

Stress-Busters for Worries about Finding Love

Of all the men in America, almost two-thirds are married. And they're obviously marrying many of the women who worry they'll never find a mate. So get off it—and enjoy your singleness while you still have the chance!

While you're enjoying being single, learn new ways of discovering and projecting your power.

Complete the following Finding Love quiz with either a True or False answer:

Finding Love

____1. The biggest obstacle to finding love is not having high enough expectations of what you deserve.

____2. The biggest mistake daters make is getting too close too soon.

____3. To avoid heartbreak, daters should become good listeners.

Scoring Key

1. <u>True</u>. When you believe you deserve to meet a quality mate, you will find one because:

<u>Gilda-Gram®</u>
We attract not whom we *want*,
but who we *are*.

2. <u>True</u>. Instead of rushing into a relationship, follow the warning, "Buyer beware." Take your time in getting to know someone thoroughly. Ask yourself: "Would I rather be with *just anyone* for the *wrong reasons,* or be *single* for the *right ones?* Immerse yourself in the activities you're passionate about. Your passion for life will attract men who are solid and secure.

3. <u>True</u>. We are blessed with two ears and one mouth, so listen twice as much as you speak. Most importantly, listen to what is not being said. What's omitted could be a vital clue about how your romance will turn out. Don't be shy about asking pointed questions. Inquire about past romances, former marriages, the way a man treats his children and parents, and what he enjoys. Look for patterns, and if stories don't jive, that's your signal to look further, or escape.

One of the saddest paradoxes in life is that those who are most desperate for love don't get it. Those who instead seek their passions find that love finds *them.* The explanation is simple: people who project an image of someone fascinated with life becomes all the more lovable.

Worry #2: Keeping Love

Carolyn was sitting by the fireplace at her best friend's Thanksgiving feast one year when she smugly announced to the women around her, "I never have to worry about Mel. He'd never cheat on me." Five years later, Mel told his devastated wife that he wanted a divorce because he had fallen in love with another woman. Her friends never let her forgot the certainty with which Carolyn had spoken those sure-sounding words. What she learned is that one can never be too sure about what life will dish us.

At some point in most relationships, most women will worry about their mate's fidelity. It may be the result of being at a party and watching her husband flirt with another woman. It may be seeing his sudden interest in chat rooms on the Internet. It may be that she notices a newfound interest he takes in his appearance. Her suspicions may be unfounded, but whatever the cue, she begins to have an eerie feeling that something might be going on while she's been taking her man for granted. And now, for the first time in a long time, she begins to take more interest in the guy she's lived with for some time.

Each gender incorporates ways of trying to keep

its spouse from cheating. Men worry more about "mate-straying" when their wife is very beautiful and much younger than they are. Women worry about their husbands cheating when their guy has a high income.

David M. Buss, Ph.D., a psychologist at the University of Texas, found that men who want to keep their wife's interest, deliberately flaunt their finances, with luxurious dining and expensive gifts. Women who worry their spouse will cheat may question his female "friendships," and become highly emotional about his flirting. Some women go to the drastic extreme of checking up on their spouse at unexpected times, with or without the help of a detective agency. And both sexes try to keep their mate's interest by enhancing their looks—and thus the increase in plastic surgery, Botox, and fillers for both genders.

Maintaining relationships is difficult because nothing in life stays the same. If a man is going through a personal crisis, he may feel the need to boost his ego with attention from ladies he wouldn't ordinarily seek. Especially if his wife is immersed in an exciting career, or dotes on their kids, she may miss the signs that her partner feels abandoned.

Since most men prefer to avoid sharing their vulnerability, many try to impress another woman, who doesn't know their flaws, rather than attempt to regain back love from their own wife, who does. Yet, since women think of themselves as the "relationship police," believing they are totally responsible for what happens in their relationships, if they do catch their husband in an indiscretion, besides being furious, they also blame themselves for not being a good enough—meaning, "perfect"—wife.

Stress-Busters for Worries about Keeping Love

Complete the following Re-Igniting Your Love quiz with either a True or False answer. It will point you towards the route to follow to maintain your love.

Re-Igniting Your Love

____1. The most frequent complaint of most couples is boredom.

____2. It is normal for the spark to go out of a relationship over time.

____3. You can check your closeness by examining your language.

Scoring Key:

1. True. Familiarity in time can breed boredom. But if two people remain interest*ed*, they will continue to be interest*ing* to each other. So whatever you do, as much in love as you think you are, don't quit your fascinating job and your invigorating hobbies just to be together.

2. True. Most marriages go through highs and lows. But if a relationship was once passionate, those embers

can still burn strong--with some work. Return to the days when you went out on dates. Recapture how it felt to look forward to seeing each other. Meet for drinks after work and flirt. Let the children know you will routinely be setting up together time, and get reliable babysitters in advance. Prepare candlelight dinners. Take long weekends away. In other words, make your love the priority it used to be when you were courting. Follow the same path that got you to walk down the aisle, and the romance will return once the steps are revisited.

3. <u>True</u>. Watch your language. Couples who see themselves as a team, use the "we" and "us" words often. They also incorporate a willingness to be open about how they feel. Women who complain that their men are emotionally shutdown must make a deliberate attempt at be open themselves because:

<u>Gilda-Gram®</u>
Self-disclosure is symmetrical.

It's a fact of relationship life that people feel closest to those with whom they share their secrets. So do that. In addition, offer your honey honest praise that makes him feel good. Flattery will get you *everywhere*. Men whose egos are stroked at home usually don't feel the need to find someone else who does.

Worry #3: Losing Love

Our culture has instilled in women that to be "successful" means that they must be a card-carrying member of Noah's Ark. Women worry that if they're no longer part of a pair, they'll be a failure in the eyes of the world. Who cares? Yet, they're concerned that they will be seen as unlovable, or too "bitchy" to keep a guy. They obsess over what to tell people. They wonder, "Will I lose face?," or "Will I be ashamed that I was dumped?," or "Will I feel bad when I see him with a new woman?" Following a fictitious script they've already written and produced, they dig themselves into a worrying frenzy.

Karen, a gorgeous psychologist, felt that her marriage of 20 years was going well. That is, until she got breast cancer and needed a double mastectomy. Suddenly, her husband was coldly telling her that he could no longer look at her newly cut up body that turned him off. Being a psychologist, Karen was aware that this was not her issue, but his. Nonetheless, it hurt her terribly, and she tried to hide her unsightly scars from him. She temporarily suspended her practice until she completed the necessary chemotherapy and had breast reconstruction.

During her terrible ordeal, she noticed some letters lying around. As she opened the one on top, she saw a love letter addressed to her husband. She discovered that her husband had been having an affair two years *before* she had even been diagnosed. And her cancer simply provided the easy out that her husband was seeking to walk out on their marriage.

Karen spent a year in intense therapy. Finally, she began to come to terms with her life. Once she felt better, she returned to work, she began writing, she started doing outreach for other cancer victims, and she began dating. When asked by others what had gone wrong in her marriage, she truthfully responded, "My husband left me for another woman."

It was now out in the open, she wasn't feeling sorry for herself, and the conversation continued from there. Karen's own comfort level with the truth was her way of handling her story, without allowing herself to wallow in past pain. As she told her tale, the reaction of most of her dates was, "What's wrong with your husband to ever want to leave *you*?"

Karen is now married to an adoring man who often thanks her ex-husband for leaving the door open for him to capture her heart. This woman's new love story could never have occurred until Karen took comfort in knowing that, despite her raw deal, she was still very special. Especially after a love loss,

Gilda-Gram®
Find comfort in your life story.

Part of your comfort is in being able to reveal your truth. Because self-disclosure IS symmetrical, the way you tell your truth sets the stage for the way others tell theirs to you. Love is far more enjoyable with someone who's come out of the dark tunnel, grown from the past, and appreciates basking in the new light.

Stress-Busters for Worries about Losing Love

If you have just suffered a love loss—whether through separation, divorce, or death—before trying to replace "him" with a new model, take a time out for yourself. It's natural to repeat the "If only" worry: "If only he was . . .;" "If only we were . . .;" "If only I had been . . ." Accept that this is the mulling over of things past that are too late to fix. Understand that your love is gone and that you will be in the more enviable position of building a new life for yourself, where you get to start all over again.

This is a refreshing phase of your life, once you realize it may take some time to sink in. Just be sure to give yourself as much time as you need to do the necessary grieving for the love you once had.

Healing After Lost Love

To accelerate your healing, resist making your

former love into an unrealistic Adonis, who was without his faults. Complete the following exercise:

1. Divide a paper into two columns. On one side list this man's positive traits; on the other, list his negative ones.
2. Divide a paper into two columns. On one side list this man's positive traits; on the other, list his negative ones.

3. List the things you will now be able to do that you couldn't or wouldn't do when he was in your life.

4. What did you learn and how did you grow from being with him?

5. How will you use this experience in the years to come?

Don't push yourself to heal faster than you're ready. Don't fall prey to friends' urging you to go out. At your own pace, slowly become involved in activities you enjoy. You'll know when you feel comfortable enough to start socializing again. Honor that, and proceed according to your own beautiful needs.

CATEGORY II
Stress in Other Relationships

Worry #4:
Friendships

All relationships, whether they are with women or men, involve two people feeling they are getting back at least some of what they are giving. Nobody wants to feel taken advantage of. When that equation becomes lopsided, something in the relationship has to give.

When two people share a life, crises, children, job pressures, and more, what often happens is that the closeness they previously shared naturally gets shaken, and an accommodation needs to occur, to re-balance the seesaw. Actually, this is the test of a strong and sustainable relationship. And this is when women, in particular, draw from the resources their friends can provide.

Women's friendships are so important to them that when they lose a close friend, they feel just as depleted as though a man had left them. Margie and Sara had been inseparable friends for about two years. They shared practically everything with each other, except their husbands. One evening, Sara went to dinner with Alana whom she liked and had not seen in several months. Margie had had a big argument with Alana several years earlier, and things were never the same for them after that.

When Margie called Sara's home that night, her husband innocently said that his wife was at dinner with Alana. Suddenly, Margie became furious, almost as though she was being cheated on. She felt that Sara should have respected her feelings about this woman by staying away from her, just as she had. Of course, Sara didn't feel the same way. If anything, she felt strangled by Margie's attempted hold on her.

Abruptly, she told Margie that their relationship couldn't continue as it had been, which left Margie feeling as though she had lost a lover. Breakups are difficult for women, no matter whom they're with.

Stress-Busters for Worries about Friendships

If either you or your friend feels taken advantage of at any time, the most important thing is to communicate your feelings. The golden rule of friendship is:

Gilda-Gram®
To keep a friend, be a friend.

If you start by giving more than you're getting,

you can always pull back. But this way, you'll have a reserve of offerings in your stash. Just don't overdo your giving in an effort to be liked—which women are more prone to doing than men. Also recognize that all friends are not created equal. While someone might not qualify as a "best" friend, she could nonetheless serve you as someone spontaneous with whom you can party at the last minute, or just a friend you can socialize with after work. Don't dismiss a friend just because it doesn't seem that you'll be buddies forever. People have both short and long-term needs. Enjoy people for whoever they are at the time you meet.

Are You a Good Friend?

1. List the things you derive from your friends.

2. How do you give back to your friends?

3. Do you ever feel taken advantage of by friends?

4. How do you communicate your feelings when the friendship equation goes out of whack?

Scoring Key

What did you discover about yourself from taking this quiz? Do you give more than you get, often leaving you feeling bad? Or, do you under-give? If so, why?

Communication is key. Women tend to ruminate over hurt emotions. Then they complain to another party, instead of taking direct action with the person who bruised them. But unless they share what's going on with the person who can make things better, they won't be healing anytime soon.

Give yourself a time limit to resolve your issues with a friend. Either decide to confront your friend, or let her—and the problem—go. After the time you've allotted, don't allow yourself to worry about your issue with this friend again. Holding onto hurt only continues to make your friendships dysfunctional. Is that really how you want to interact with people you enjoy?

Worry #5:
Children

Women worry about their children no matter how old they are. But a recent finding suggests that a woman's worry can affect the health of her baby, if she is pregnant. It can also affect the baby's subsequent health as an adult. A study at the University of Kentucky College of Medicine found that stressed mothers could retard the growth of their fetus, and deliver their babies prematurely. Low birth weight correlates with hypertension in adults and above-average death rates from heart attacks. So the worry a mother feels while carrying her young can determine the health the offspring enjoys when he reaches adulthood.

Even when children are a few years old, women know that no matter how supportive a partner they have, it is they who do the majority of worrying about them. Mothers worry about everything, from the kind of cereal they give their kids, to the toys they buy them.

The National Institute of Child Health and Human Development found that a baby's first four months are when baby and mother develop the attachment that teaches each to read the other's expressions, so to provide caretaking during those months is not advisable. After that period, however, a child can benefit from the socializing he gets at day care. But no matter what a mother chooses to do, even if her family can afford to hire support staff, it is still she who must coordinate all their actions.

Crystal was doing very well as the owner of her own Public Relations firm. She had taken great pains in building up her business to where she now had a respectable following of clients. Her husband, Ted, was a lawyer for a large city hospital. They had two bright sons who were in their teens. Suddenly, Crystal was receiving calls from her older son's school telling her that he was continuously involved in fights with other students.

When Ted arrived home that night, they discussed how they would handle their son. Ted recommended that Crystal abandon her business and return to being a full-time mother. Crystal was furious that it was she who had to change her entire life around, while Ted continued his life exactly the way it had always been. She was now bringing home a high salary, and she had become a major financial contributor to the household. What was Ted thinking?

Often parents say, "Little children, little problems; big children, big problems." Especially with all the school shootings, parents are becoming more concerned about school incidents their kids report to them. It used to be sticks and stones will break my bones. Now it's guns and knives, leaving parents terrified. Today's parents are being sued for what their children do. So many are becoming more involved in overseeing their kids, including on the Internet.

Stress-Busters for Worries about Children

This is a universal worry for all parents. Some ways to keep your kids safe include the following:

1. Form communities with other parents so you have a support system.

2. Investigate what your child does with his free time. You don't have to read your kid's diary, but know, at least, that she keeps private notes in one.

3. Fifty-three percent of teens have come across offensive web sites that deal with pornography, hate groups, and violence, which they say come to them inadvertently, while they were doing other activities online. Parents should use Internet service providers that filter out inappropriate messages they want their kids to avoid.

4. Ask questions about "foreign" objects you find in your child's room. One mother asked her son about some unfamiliar pieces of metal on his shelf. He shrugged nonchalantly, "They're shotgun shells." They were out of that house immediately. Another time, the same boy came home with a wrist-mounted slingshot. The

mother asked, "Is it legal for you to have this?" He said, "Sure." Not quite sure herself, she marched down to her local police precinct, slingshot in hand, and discovered that these were illegal for kids under 16. When she returned home and confronted her son, he typically said, "But Tommy's parents allow him to have one." Her response of, "Tough" accompanied her removal of this, too, from his possession.

Finally, this little darling said he wanted her to get him a Beebe gun because his friend had just gotten one. This mother called her son's friend's mother who rationalized to her, "A Beebe gun is a good device for hand-eye coordination." The mother glibly asked, "What happened to basketball?"

Parents today may be more hip than the parents of previous generations, but they are also more involved in their own lives. Women who must work simply can't be there for their kids, and this opens the door for their kids to get into trouble. Nonetheless, parents must return to being parents. Little kids and teens alike need supervision by someone. If we oversee our children, no matter how old they are, we will be able to keep our own worries at bay! Make this your rule of thumb:

Gilda-Gram®
Be friendly towards, not friends with, your children.

This way, you'll be able to keep abreast of what your kids are doing, and also be able to discipline them when it's necessary. But don't expect worry to automatically cease as soon as your kids are adults. As I write these words, my friend, Leila, is on the phone with her 30-year-old daughter who is in the middle of a bitter divorce. Although mother and daughter live 3,000 miles apart, Leila is having trouble sleeping, as she worries about how her daughter will make it through this ordeal. Mothers forever worry about their children! ☺

Worry #6:
Parents

In the first study in a decade of how terminally ill patients are cared for, the National Institutes of Health found that it's usually a woman in the family--be it wife, sister, or daughter--who provides the nursing care. Most elderly are not in nursing homes, and American Demographics concurred that nearly 3/4 of informal elder-care providers are women: 29 percent are daughters, 23 percent are wives, and 20 percent are other females. Yet, rarely are the needs of these caregiver women addressed. Unfortunately, the study also found that while these women helped dying family members, when they themselves were dying, they were left to have to hire paid help.

Former North Carolina Senator, Elizabeth Dole, herself the wife of a wounded World War II hero, founded The Elizabeth Dole Foundation for caregivers to wounded warriors. She had gotten the idea when her own husband, former Kansas senator, Bob Dole, was being treated at Walter Reed Medical Center in Bethesda, Maryland in 2010. The beds around him were filled with veterans of the wars in Afghanistan and Iraq, and these veterans depended on family caregivers to recuperate.

Women seem to learn to be nurturers from the time they are young. I remember when I was sick one day, and my 7-year-old stepdaughter was visiting. She immediately asked if she could make me some hot tea to get me to feel better. I thought, "How sweet this child is!" I wondered whether I would have seen this kind of kindness if she had been a 7-year-old "he."

Therefore, it's no surprise that whether their parents are young or old,

Gilda-Gram®
**Daughters are usually
the designated worriers about their parents.**

As a 10-year-old child, when I became separated from my grandmother in a large department store in which we were shopping, my concern was not for myself, but for her, because I knew she suffered from dizzy spells. When we become older, and we accept the role of caregiver for our parents, it is not without a cry to our brothers that "she's your mother, too." But even when a mother-in-law is infirm, it is often the woman who *married into the family*, not the mother's son, who takes charge.

Melanie grew up in a house marked by her parents' fighting. One night, after her mother found out her dad was having an affair, and she confronted him, her father beat her. She lay in a corner, crying and bleeding. After all the years of observing this, teenage Melanie took it upon herself to call the cops, who quickly hauled her dad off to jail. She admits that she had always considered herself her mother's keeper.

Years later, the memory of her role in her father's incarceration stays with her. Although her parents are divorced now, and her mom is remarried, 24-year-old Melanie, successfully out on her own, can't have lasting relationships with men because of her need to mother—or, "smother" them. Her excuse is that she fears these guys will turn out like her dad.

It's bad enough to be a caregiver while growing up, but being the overseer of an elderly parent has ramifications that leave adult women feeling exhausted and guilty over abandoning their own families. In addition, studies find that these women often experience physical, verbal or emotional ill treatment from those they care for who are themselves frustrated over being so dependent.

The typical caregiver is a 46-year-old woman who cares for her 77-year-old mother that lives alone nearby, and has a chronic illness. Although the daughter is employed, she spends 18 hours per week caring for her mom. Forty-one percent of these caregivers are also raising children under 18. This arrangement generally lasts for 4.5 years. During that time, half the caregivers surveyed reported taking off from work, coming in late, working fewer hours, giving up work entirely, or taking early retirement.

A major problem is that caregivers don't often talk about feeling frustrated, isolated, and alone. It makes them feel guilty about resenting those who raised them and sacrificed for them. Not sharing their feelings is unusual for women because most tend to want to talk about pressing issues, at least with close friends. But they are overwhelmed by how their once-strong parents have turned into frail bodies that are now almost unrecognizable. These women often don't know how to *process* their feelings about their new, reversed roles, much less *discuss* them.

Stress-Busters for Worries about Parents

The U.S. elderly population is expected to grow to 80 million people by the year 2050, and most of the caregivers will probably continue to be daughters. Since there is no formalized system in place for taking care of our parents, and the idea of placing them in dispassionate nursing homes is horrifying to most children, baby boomers feel great pressure and guilt about being the "sandwich" generation between their aging parents and their growing offspring, all of who put demands on them.

As our population lives longer, and subsequently must deal with the accompanying disabilities of growing older, the female caregivers must develop coping mechanisms that allow them to continue living their own lives amid their chaos. Follow the Dr. Gilda Caregiver Coping Plan, to bust these worries up:

1. <u>Grieve for the person you once knew</u>, who is no longer the same as he or she once was. Give yourself permission to feel sad that your parent is no longer the same person he or she once was.

2. <u>Accept that you're doing the best you can</u> to make your parent's life as comfortable as possible.

3. <u>Think about what would happen</u> if you were not available to provide your input. Be grateful for how much better off your parent is because of you.

4. <u>Devote time to yourself</u>, no matter what else is happening around you. Make some special time all your own to enjoy *without guilt*.

    Get into these feel-good habits now. Be sure you feel totally grounded, as your parents become a greater and greater responsibility. Your incentive to stay centered is in knowing that your parent is depending on you to be healthy and strong. You truly are making a difference!

CATEGORY III.
Health, Looks, & Finances

Worry #7:
Physical Health

In Freud's time, when women complained about various health issues, they were quickly categorized as "hysterical hypochondriacs." Often, for lack of concerned medical support, these women felt guilty that they had not done enough to prevent their disease. As they continued to monitor their health and gripe about their long time in getting well, they had bouts of depression. Today, women's depression occurs so frequently, it is called the "common cold of mental illness."

Sadly, things have changed only somewhat from Freud's era. We're more conscientious about our health, we're more knowledgeable about what we can do to prevent many diseases, and we have easy and immediate access to the latest scientific data. More than 60 percent of adults say they take a vitamin or nutritional supplement daily. In fact, the worldwide market for dietary supplements and natural remedies is worth about $65 billion, the United States representing 60 percent of that total. We boast health sites on the Internet, health food stores on practically every metropolitan street corner, disease prevention programs, books, tapes for nearly every ailment, and celebrity tell-alls that disclose real personal suffering and their miracle cures. About 86 percent of Americans say they exercise, with 65 percent of these exercisers admitting they do it to stay healthy. But too much knowledge can be a dangerous thing. With all this focus on what we can and should do, one must wonder if we're not becoming overly paranoid about our health.

One of women's health worries is whether to have a baby and when. Single women in their thirties and forties have increased anxiety because the likelihood of conceiving and delivering a healthy baby declines with age. What if they can't find a partner who's interested? Some single women want to become mothers so badly, they end up partnering with inappropriate mates, just to father their kids. Others choose simply to adopt and raise a child on their own. Women who are married and have anxiety over not conceiving often spend thousands of dollars on fertility treatments.

Physical safety is another health worry for women today. Since news reporting tends to highlight blood and gore, women glumly note the increasing rise in rapes and murders. Some of our most popular TV shows detail how women are overtaken by various brutes. Terrified women resort to carrying guns, while others learn methods of self-defense. There is a great need for women to change their state of fear, to feel stronger about their physical being, and to set up security contacts, so they know they are protected in case of a crisis.

But of all the panic attacks caused by health worries, probably the scariest concern for women today is breast cancer, even though heart disease ranks as the Number One killer of women. From the pink ribbon that everyone can identify as a symbol of the disease, to the barrage of terrifying statistics in the media, the fear of breast cancer is on most women's minds. It has them questioning everything they can safely ingest, wear, and do, and it causes a great deal of confusion.

For example, some studies point to wine as good for the heart, while others suggest it may lead to increased risk of breast cancer. Now, even the chemicals in professional lawn care and dry-cleaning services are being scrutinized as possible contributors to the disease. What is all right to eat, drink, and clean with? One can't be too sure, as one day something is named "unsafe," while another day, that same thing is considered to be okay.

Familiar with the one-in-nine breast cancer statistic, rather than looking forward to getting a clean bill of health each year, many women instead experience so-called "white-coat hypertension," or high blood pressure, whenever they are even in the presence of a physician. More fearful women are doing breast exams almost daily, while others are postponing their annual mammograms completely. Finally, breast cancer researchers are admitting that while trying to raise awareness about the disease, they've scared most women into a panic.

Actually, breast cancer isn't as lethal as most women believe. The one-in-nine statistic is even misleading. It does not mean that out of nine women standing on line, one will contract the disease. Instead, it refers to a woman's risk of developing breast cancer over her entire lifetime, assuming that she lives to 85. If she's thirty, that means one in 5,900; if she's fifty, that means one in 590; if she's eighty, that means one in 290.

If breast cancer is detected early, the five-year survival rate is more than 95 percent. While the rate of breast cancer rose steeply through the 1980's, now that more women are getting mammograms, and the examining equipment has become ever more sophisticated, the increase has stopped, and the numbers have remained steady since 1990.

Another health worry for a segment of the female population is whether to take Estrogen Replacement Therapy. It's been nearly a century since women began living long enough to experience hot flashes, night sweats, and mood swings. Yet, we are no closer to knowing what to do about them than we were then.

Historically, women were excluded from clinical studies; medical schools cut off the breasts of female cadavers because they interfered with "more important" organs. Changes in bones, blood, heart, brain, bladder, and kidneys as a result of estrogen deprivation were not studied. So today's medical community does not know how to deal with women at the close of their reproductive cycles—and we're playing catch-up. This is particularly perplexing when almost 50 million women, or 20 percent of the U.S. population, could be having a hot flash today!

Who should take estrogen, for how long, and at what risk? While the hormone is believed to be an aid in osteoporosis, Alzheimer's, high cholesterol, and heart disease, it is also said to correlate with breast, uterine and ovarian cancer, and with blood clots. So is a woman to take the drug and get cancer, or does she not, and suffer other ailments in a nursing home? The question is whether estrogen replacement therapy really reduces the risk of stroke, heart failure, and brittle bones. The recommendation continues to be, "Check with your doctor." But the reality has women asking, "What does HE know?" These contradictions are enough to stress any woman out.

And women are, indeed, stressed out. In a study of 30,000 people conducted by Roper Starch Worldwide, it was found that women around the world, in all social and economic categories, and especially mothers, are likely to be stressed. Of all the groups studied, full-time working mothers with children under thirteen report the greatest stress. Family, work, and money are some of the most common complaints, but a survey by a candle company, Illuminations, found that 51 percent of respondents felt stressed even watching Martha Stewart on TV *where everything works perfectly.*

Gilda-Gram®
**The desire to be *everything* to *everyone*
is a main female worry.**

Aiming for impossible perfection in their homes and relationships, women therefore needlessly set themselves up for disappointment.

Stress-Busters for Worries about Physical Health

Women can try to do as much as they know to do to prevent disease and the stress it brings. But whether we've contracted a disease or not, it is essential that we live our lives positively. One such positive role model was Rita, a young, 52-year-old widow, who said that having lupus was the best thing that happened to her. She had been dating a difficult, critical man. After her diagnosis, she took charge. She called her boyfriend and immediately ended their relationship. Now she jokes, "If not for my disease, this guy might have given me a stroke, from which I would have died. Thank you, lupus; I'm alive, well, and once again in control of my life."

Gilda-Gram®
Everything that happens *to* us, happens *for* us.

As Rita discovered, it's just up to each of US to find out

what that "for" is!!

Become a Wellness Wonder Chick

To repeat, no matter what happens, strong women know,

Gilda-Gram®
**When something happens TO you,
it really happens FOR you.**

To do something FOR yourself, follow the Dr. Gilda 3-Steps to Positivity:

1. <u>Feel sorry for yourself for only a pre-set period of time.</u> After that period, refuse to allow your emotions to rule you. Set up appointments with friends you've lost touch with, investigate activities you've never tried before, and return to the things you once enjoyed. Generally, if you kick yourself in the shins, you forget that your head has been hurting.

2. <u>Don't ask "Why, me?" Instead ask, "What am I supposed to learn from this?</u> Consider whatever "bad luck" you just had as a schoolroom lesson meant to provide you with insight about how to enhance your life from this day forward. Thus, turn your alleged "bad luck" into a "good luck" message. You are not your ailment. Get off the victim platform.

3. <u>Decide how you'll use this experience to improve your life.</u> Make a list of the good things you have going for you. Pursue the dreams you haven't yet accomplished.

Everything happens for a reason. If you worry about becoming ill, but have not, consider yourself really lucky. But if you do contract an illness, know this:

<u>Gilda-Gram®</u>
Whatever happens,
I will handle it.

Whatever happened, make it the first step to enhancing the rest of your life.

Worry #8: Finances

Money issues worry women. A Money Magazine survey found that women worry about money more than men do, and, sixty percent admitted that they think more about their personal finances than about sex! One statistic reveals that women worry about money 70 percent of the time, and a whopping 55 percent said they worry about it *all* the time.

One reason for women's money worries may be because in 80 percent of American homes, money handling is the woman's job. And as time goes on, because of divorce and life expectancy, it will be the sole responsibility for 80 to 90 percent of all women.

Most women are not taught money management skills. When my dad died, my college-educated mother, who actually handled my father's business for him, still didn't know how to balance her own checkbook! The learned helplessness of women during my mother's era was passed down to me. Unfortunately, it took me having to go through myriad male stockbrokers and losing a huge amount of money under their care until I became money smart. More and more women are becoming money savvy. Time Magazine reported that in the last twenty years, women are leading the way in philanthropy and fundraising by 180%, with more than half of all charitable foundations now being run by females. This points to the independence with which women are now leading their lives. But a third of mature adults were poor in the '60s, and there is still the memory—and subsequent worry—of becoming impoverished again.

The worry over financial security is not limited to older women, however. A study commissioned by the more youthful Self Magazine found that women still feel guilt over spending time and money on themselves. Most of the women surveyed said they want to enjoy their lives, but few feel they do. While 40 percent are willing to buy an expensive dinner, and 28 percent will purchase a costly outfit, an overwhelming 69 percent said they still feel at a loss as to how to manage their finances.

Gilda-Gram®
Money is power.
Women who lack money savvy also lack power.

Many women grew up learning that number crunching was a man's business, and even if their moms managed the family's finances, overseeing the *big* money at work was their dad's job, because he was, after all, the "powerful" one. Even in today's world, the man's career usually assumes greater importance either because it has begun as the better-paying job, or because the woman must take at least some time out for child rearing. In most relationships, to claim her power, a woman either has to begin the partnership on equal economic footing, or negotiate later to claim it—which often erupts into angry discourse.

Most couples are in a tizzy about how to deal with the division of money. Some experts find that it's the man who wants to merge a couple's money, while the woman wants to separate it. Estimates suggest that 80 percent of couples actually do merge their finances. But other experts warn that for a marriage to survive, there must be financial independence for each partner to feel his or her identity.

Nobody knows for sure what the equitable thing to do is. But most couples can describe endless arguments about money. In the meantime, women continue to lack the know-how to take charge of their money. While many feel they're underpaid at work, they're too passive either to ask for a raise, or to move to another position. In addition, women are often impulsive buyers, purchasing items when they feel depressed or unfulfilled in other areas of their life, even though they don't know how they're going to pay for them when the bill arrives.

Finally, too many young women blankly dismiss their company's information regarding IRA's, 401K plans, and insurance policies, because it seems too far down the road to be of concern. Add these factors to women's history of being financially dependent on men (which they confuse for love), and the guilt they feel about spending money on themselves, and we find that, despite women's increasingly upward mobility in the work world, money worries continue to run them ragged.

Money confusion is also vividly seen on the singles scene. The current dating dilemma is, "Who should pay on a date?" Does it depend on who asks whom out? Does it depend on who the higher wage earner is? A "Sex in the City" episode had the female characters pondering whether to buy or rent an apartment to live in. Charlotte revealed that she'd rather rent, saying, "If I meet a man who rents when I own, it would be emasculating. Men don't want a woman who's too self-sufficient." This is an old comedy series, but the fear of emasculating your man with your greater assets still boldly exists.

Women don't need a TV series to prove what they already know is the golden rule of money:

Gilda-Gram®
Whoever has the money has the power.

As old as this popular TV series was, Sex and the City's Charlotte was right: if it's *she* who has the money—and the power—it's *he* who feels dominated—and he's likely to run. No matter which century or culture we're in, a man who feels overpowered by his woman's finances, often also feels controlled—and that's a dirty relationship word!

Rona, a woman in her sixties, dated Paul of the same age. Since they agreed that they were both living on fixed incomes, they said they'd split the expenses on each date. But after a year of this, Rona became resentful when she saw Paul shell out large sums of money for things she considered frivolous, while he had his hand out to her for her share of dinners and movies. Though they were not even married, their relationship soon came to a screeching halt when they could not settle their money disputes.

These days, there's a new syndrome surfacing among divorced men. In record numbers, guys are seeking women with assets—for the same reasons women have historically sought rich guys. These male bounty hunters cry "onedownsmanship."

Instead of following the centuries-old custom of flashing their resources, they bemoan their poverty due to their alimony and child support. They convince ladies to lavish *them* with money and gifts. And many sympathetic female financiers are so lonely, they welcome the sweet-talking seducers. Unfortunately, the women discover later that they've given their hearts for superficial love—and they are furious.

Many of today's marriages have changed from the days when a wife stayed home, while her husband worked. American families now consist of dual-working spouses, where the woman might even out-earn her mate. The 1998 U.S. Bureau of the Census showed that a whopping 25--30 percent of women earned more than their husbands. This percentage continues to rise, and today, one third of all marriages consist of wives as the dominant wage earner. But no statistics describe how a couple successfully manages these inequitable earning ratios. Anthropologist Helen Fischer explains away today's high divorce rate with two words: "working woman."

A 24-year-old male college student of mine agreed that it would bother him if his woman earned more than he because he wants to be "the provider." A 30-year-old guy sitting next to him agreed.

For four years, a 40-year-old female client of mine willfully hid from her husband the large amount of money she earned. When I told her that marriage should be based on trust and honesty, she insisted that she wanted to protect her husband's fragile ego. The following year, they were divorced.

A 30-year-old female college student, returning to school to complete her bachelor's degree, announced that she had just been dumped by her high-school-graduate boyfriend. He told her, "I want a less successful woman. I don't want competition." Wow!! Sex in the City's Charlotte was on point about the male intimidation factor.

So how do women achieve their goals of personal success, along with their dreams of everlasting love? It certainly seems that succeeding professionally and finding love are two conflicting objectives.

Clara was leaving on an exciting business trip, one that she had been looking forward to for quite some time. She believed that this was the trip that would get her boss to finally recognize the hard work she had done on the company's major account. She knew that this was her week to shine. Tom, her husband of 12 years, had just lost his job, and was now left at home.

Gilda-Gram®
No man likes to wait,
because it puts him out of control.

On this morning, Tom watched his wife prepare to leave. He studied her as she carefully put on her makeup and took her suit out of the plastic from the dry cleaner. As Clara was opening the door, she noticed the forlorn look on her husband's face. No doubt, she felt sorry for him for having just lost his job. But instead of wishing her luck, he shot some nasty words at her, questioning the location of the big pot he needed to cook the roast she had prepared for him while she was gone. She felt bad that she hadn't heard any encouragement from him; after all, he *knew* this was an important trip for her.

Nonetheless, out of typical female guilt, Clara phoned Tom four times from her cell phone before she boarded her plane. Then, although she was working and networking as hard as she could during her trip, her entire week away was marked by stress and worry.

When she called Tom each evening after dinner, he was cold and dispassionate. Their conversations were punctuated with Tom's accusations and criticisms that Clara had not left enough food for him, had not filled the car's gas tank, and had not paid several of the outstanding bills. He continued to ask her when he could expect her home, and what she wanted to do during the weekend. All she could think of was her need to spend the weekend catching up on sleep.

Clara felt a tug at her stomach. She actually felt guilty when her boss finally offered her the promotion she had been hoping for. Unbelievably, her biggest worry was how to break the good news to Tom! The couple is now divorced.

Not every couple in love immediately opts for wedded bliss. According to the Census Bureau, the trend is that more than half of all couples live together before marriage, with unmarried couples making up ten percent of adult American households. Presumably, this gives two people plenty of time to work out their money issues before they decide to tie the knot.

But many couples have no intention of ever walking down the aisle. Without a marital plan, these couples avoid setting up important financial arrangements. Love blinds even the most levelheaded, and before many people realize it, they own joint property with little protection in case they break up or in the event one of the partners dies.

Even after a couple marries, money issues are still at the top of the list of marital disputes. That goes back to the fact that money is a symbol of power, and power struggles are part of most people's married lives. But whether married or not, living together is more than divvying up whose job it is to take out the trash. If one mate feels overtaxed, while the other is allegedly getting a free ride, there's need for negotiation.

Gilda-Gram®
Continuous renegotiation of roles is what marks a good marriage.

Renegotiation of roles and resources is a constant requirement when two people are growing. If mates are not growing, boredom sets in. So, really, what's the alternative? To avoid boredom, sophisticated negotiation techniques are necessary to settle financial issues and the emotional strains that develop from them. If two people can't do this on their own, it's time to find help!

Stress-Busters for Worries about Finances

Just because money is a symbol of power does not mean a couple should use it as part of its arsenal. If each mate were to pull his or her own weight, one adult should not need to consult the other about spending money on personal pleasure. But the key words here are "each mate must pull his or her own weight."

A prevalent female mindset is that a woman should strive for personal and professional advancement—only until she becomes hitched. This philosophy cuts across all socioeconomic groups and ages:

Dear Dr. Gilda:
 I'm a legal secretary who is paid quite well. My boyfriend and I have been together for three years, and he has recently asked me to marry him. We're both 34. He is very generous, and because he has a booming business, I will never have to worry about financial security.
 The problem is that I'm also in love with a man I've known all my life. This other man left college before graduation in order to support his family. He makes an adequate salary, but with him I know that I'll always have to work to help support us. I feel like I love two men, and I'm very confused.
Sallyann

Dear Sallyann,
 No matter what you do, don't marry anyone at this time. Just because you seem chronologically ready

for marriage, emotionally, you are out to sea. You're weighing which of these two guys will be the better provider, not which will make the most loving mate. This was the way women thought decades ago, but it's not the healthiest way for you to be thinking now.

Just because Guy #1 has a booming business at this time does not guarantee that his business will continue to soar forever. If he were to go bankrupt, will you still want to maintain the marriage? Surely, then you'd have to return to work.

Realize your own worth. If you don't already love your job, find one you do love. Meanwhile, understand that when a woman marries, the agreement should provide her with more than financial security. If you can't decide which of the two men is the better for you, you don't deserve to be with either of them.

Dr. Gilda

Although there can never be a perfect 50/50 split of responsibility, if a relationship includes honest discussions about how two people will handle their finances, *and each person shares his or her worries,* the relationship has a better chance of thriving. But:

<u>Gilda-Gram®</u>
Before entering a financial arrangement, know your personal sense of money.

For Single Gals:

1. Review your earliest recollections of money. Were they positive or negative? Did you hear your parents fighting over it, or did you see them peacefully negotiating compromises? Note whether you have patterned your own money behaviors after theirs, or whether you have deliberately done the opposite.

2. Take total responsibility for understanding your money, including your investments and debts. If you have been money-reckless, immediately begin to change your ways.

3. Draw up a will.

4. Grant someone power of attorney, allowing that person to make financial decisions for you, if you become incompetent.

5. Regularly balance your checkbook, and know where all your money goes each month.

6. If you're in debt, be aggressive about getting out of it. Take your first steps today.

For Coupled Gals:

7. If you are part of an unwed couple living together, have legal papers drawn up to declare yourselves either "joint owners" with rights of survivorship" or "tenants in common." "Joint ownership means that

you and your lover own the property, and one of you will inherit it if the other one dies. "Tenants in common" means that each person owns a half share of the residence, and if one dies, half the property goes to his or her next of kin.

8. Whether you're part of an unwed couple or married, expect money issues to crop up occasionally. If you don't yet know how to fight fair with money, follow these steps:

   a) Be aware if certain issues continue to form predictable patterns that need to be addressed. If so, call them to the attention of your partner.

Gilda-Gram®
Air your worries honestly with your mate.

Let your partner know the money behaviors you admire in him, and be sure to list more of his positive traits than negative ones. Without getting angry or defensive, invite him to offer his concerns about your money management style. Then find mutually beneficial solutions.

   b) Create goals of the things you want to achieve in your relationship. Agree on how you will earn and save the money to meet these goals. Set tentative dates for accomplishing each goal, realizing that these dates are elastic, and they can be changed as you gain more insight or resources.

As soon as you recognize your power, you will realize that you have a multitude of choices.

<u>Gilda-Gram®</u>
**Either you will take charge of your money,
or your money will take charge of you.**

Worry #9: Feeling Attractive

I recently saw a headline that beautiful, young Kate Hudson is starting to melt down over her slowing career. It is believed that the 36-year-old is "worried" about losing one role after another to younger actresses.

What happens when all you've been used to getting has been based on your looks and charm? What happens when that standard is suddenly looked upon as being worthless for public consumption? While the average person is not prone to such scrutiny, Hollywood personalities are—and it's extremely stressful. Every extra wrinkle, year, and pound can set the beauty "judges" scrambling for someone else to play a role. Who are these judges that have so much pull over someone's life?

Standards of beauty in every culture differ, some calling for large, rotund shapes, and others admiring thinness. In many non-Western countries, obesity is viewed as preferable, because it is a sign of fertility and prosperity, both of which point to human survival. For example, in African cultures, fat is symbolic of maturity, fertility, wealth, and wisdom. But Western society promotes widespread distain for fat. Fat people have lower rates of college acceptance, less likelihood of being hired for jobs, and lower wages. While strong economic, psychological, and social sanctions are levied against fat men, overweight sanctions for women are more severe.

A survey of 2,000 teenage girls by Seventeen Magazine online found that 46 percent were unhappy with their bodies, 35 percent would consider plastic surgery, including breast augmentation, and 7.4 percent suffered from eating disorders.

Gilda-Gram®
**Feeling attractive suggests personal worth.
Feeling unattractive suggests low self-esteem.**

Such female preoccupations with beauty thus could create serious physical health problems, including eating disorders, overweight conditions, excessive exercise (sometimes called "exercise bulimia"), and other self-punishing behaviors. And, of course, findings support that the more women worry about the way they look, the less mental energy they have for other things.

Body image problems are not limited to middle class or white women. A study of young Native American women found that 74 percent were trying to lose weight, and research conducted through Essence Magazine showed that 65 percent of the women surveyed were dieting. In every ethnic group, adolescent girls are especially affected by body image, and it is estimated that half of them consider themselves to be "fat," and they are on diets.

Few women in our society admit to loving their bodies. A Glamour Magazine survey revealed that out of 33,000 respondents, 85 percent felt dissatisfied with their physique. Consider that no babies are born with eating disorders. They cry when they're hungry, and push their bottles away when they're full. They love their bodies as they touch themselves everywhere, suck their toes, giggle, and wave their arms. So when do those positive feelings fade? When was the first time you began to compare yourself with others who you decided were prettier, skinnier, and more attractive than you?

One study found that 70 percent of the women who looked at the beautiful models in the fashion magazines became depressed. Of course, anyone would get depressed if she compared herself to the perfect tiny shapes, cellulite-free thighs, unblemished skin, and silky, no-bad-hair-day tresses, breezing stress-free in gorgeous settings. Even though we know the truth about photoshopping, we refuse to accept that these images are unrealistic, computerized, and airbrushed to look perfect. Young girls continue to ask me why they don't look like the models on the covers of their magazines. Yes, even for older women, we still tell ourselves we want to be like "them." Well, who are *they*?

These days, being attractive in Western society, especially according to women themselves, means having a wafer-thin stick figure. This is even though most men prefer some meat on their ladies' bones. The American diet industry spends $33 billion per year on trying to get women to conform to their fake magazine models. In fact, models have been accused of *causing* eating disorders—to which Cindy Crawford tartly responded, "Do you look at pictures of me and want to puke?" But twenty years ago, models weighed 8 percent less than the average woman; today they weigh 23 percent less. No wonder the thinning of America boasts a rate of 7 million American girls and women suffering from eating disorders and the mental health problems that go with them!

We're taught that regardless of all our other achievements, we are failures if we're not young, flawless, able-bodied, and above all, thin.

Methodically, women's self-worth is chiseled away, repackaged in the form of myriad products to build it back up, and then resold to the American public, only too anxious to pay for them. All this to the tune of $10 billion dollars a year—and climbing!

Can happiness come in a bottle? In addition to the assorted tubs and tubes of war paint we apply, we invest $300 million with the cosmetic surgery industry—to get the current "look." One year, the American Society of Plastic and Reconstructive Surgeons reports that 44,000 women opted for breast implant removal, but 84 percent of those women had new implants reinserted. Many women are turning to liposuction as a means of weight-reduction. But it wasn't always this way.

During the early 1800s, it was the full-figured rubenesque physique that was popular. In the 1890s, the preference was for the slimmer, more athletic Gibson Girl. That was followed by the even thinner flapper, until the depression of the 1930s called for sturdier and chunkier females.

After World War II, at the start of the baby boomer era, Audrey Hepburn's body made most women feel fat. But that was nothing in comparison to the 1960s when Twiggy weighed in at only 89 pounds. Today, thin has become the ideal.

Model Carol Alt once said in People Magazine, "Anyone who thinks that society pressures women to live up to our image should think of what we have to go through to maintain that image." That is so true. Many models and actresses admit that every day is a battle to keep from eating.

From Pamela Anderson, who allegedly had a contract with "Baywatch" that forbade her to gain weight, to Oprah Winfrey whose battle of the bulge has infiltrated millions of homes, diet-consciousness is a reality. No matter who they are, few of the two billion women in the world can measure up to the stunning standards of ten famous supermodels and a handful of gorgeous movie stars that, in addition to starving themselves, have also been nipped, tucked, and liposucked. Yet, young girls continue to vie for the plastic Barbie-like measurements that, in real life, would be too disproportional to allow a woman to even walk!

But there's a dichotomy here. As much as a large segment of Americans yearn to resemble images of the undernourished, another segment is growing heavier. A study in the Journal of the American Medical Association finds that 55 percent of Americans are too heavy, and continuing to spread. A Harris Poll confirms that three out of four adults admit to being heavier than their "normal" weight. In 1994, 69 percent of adults exceeded their recommended weight, but in 1998, the percentage soared to 76 percent! And it is still soaring! What is happening?

We are told that Americans ate more ice cream in 1997 than the global average of two gallons per person. Maybe that's a clue—but it doesn't explain the cause. The percentage of people who are obese (thirty plus pounds overweight) has increased drastically and dangerously in every state, in both sexes, and across all age groups. Some of the biggest increases occur among 18 to 29-year-olds and among Hispanics. This is a serious matter since obesity contributes to 300,000 deaths a year, only exceeded by smoking. So how can we possibly have two such opposite beauty forces? Is the obese population simply reacting to the pressures of the weight-conscious? Or does this segment of the population simply not care about their looks and health?

<u>Gilda-Gram®</u>
**Even if we maintain our bodies,
we won't stop aging.**

Women know that the older we get, the more invisible we become. Yet with a collective spending power of $900+ billion a year, the baby boomer generation is not only historically the most resistant group to accept growing old, it is also willing to spend whatever it takes to preserve its youth.

Marketers are taking no chances on missing out on all the available dollars people have to preserve their attractiveness. With the push towards women's independence, the marketing of beauty products has changed its slant. The craze is no longer to standardize women's fashion mores from unknown sources, but to play up a woman's individual personality traits and empowerment. "Create your own beauty" is the new mantra, suggesting that it's not the industry that is dictating our beauty choices any longer; it is we! The message demands that we examine our own body types, rather than the ideals, accept them as beautiful, and make the most of them. That means that we must appreciate our body, even though it may not be the one worshiped by the fashion gurus. The new wave is to value yourself for who you are. Do you value yourself that way?

Stress-Busters for Worries about Feeling Attractive

Forget about the notion of "creating your own beauty." Instead,

Gilda-Gram®
Create a soul that loves you.

Nobody's perfect—and it's time to love yourself, warts and whatever. Without trying to be Rembrandt, draw a simple picture of yourself in the space below:

Now answer these questions to the following Self-Love Quiz:

1. Do you like the "self" you just drew?

2. If so, are you positive, confident, and self-caring? If not, what would you change? Draw an image you like better.

3. List the positive and negative words you have heard others use about you.

4. How did you feel about these words when you heard them?

5. How do you feel about yourself now?

The Self-Love Quiz will show you how independent you are of your culture's demands that you keep a certain level of attractiveness. If you're not happy with your responses, find out why. It's YOUR body, and it's YOUR feelings about yourself. Enjoy who you are, so you can project a person that is confident.

<u>Gilda-Gram®</u>
Confidence attracts
the best mates and the best jobs.

Worry #10:
Being Alone

Many women worry that they'll be alone--on weekend, at an event, at a restaurant, for their entire life. Although many women misconstrue that they are nothing without a man, no relationship can survive unless both partners first feel whole. Many relationships fail because one or both partners think they will find salvation in the other. The fact is that two needy people just can't be there for one another when each is looking to be rescued themselves. Few women realize that:

Gilda-Gram®
**It's sometimes rejuvenating
to be a single bookend.**

Women's lives are so inundated with people, information, and demands, we often forget to take a breather to figure out the next steps that are best for US. Vacations are supposed to get us to vacate. Yet, how many women take time to vacate their own lives? Women won't take the needed breather until they are totally free from all their demands.

Alone time is necessary before, during, and especially at the end of a relationship, when a woman must re-discover her identity without a mate.

<u>Gilda-Gram®</u>
Alone time is a gift you give yourself.

Without being alone, you won't be able to request what you need and expect from others. This is your period to assess your greatest qualities.

A woman is not what she *does*, or what she *gives* to others, but who she is when she is alone. Worrying about being alone only prolongs the work you need to do to discover your true assets. You must discover your assets. Otherwise, it will be too late after you're involved with someone else.

<u>Stress-Busters for Worries about Being Alone</u>

Most women put their own needs on the back burner, only to fall off the stove. Alone time gives you the opportunity to pursue activities that you have otherwise abandoned. On the following list of 6 Life-Enhancing Passions, circle the ones you neglect.

1. Health
2. Social
3. Self-Improvement

4. Spiritual
5. Financial
6. Family

Decide why you neglect any of the six above. What are you missing by omitting them from your life? Are you ready to give yourself balance by including every single one of these in your new goals?

Now write how you will fulfill at least one dream in each of these categories. To ensure your promise, enter the date that you will begin.

Take This Dare

During your alone time, step outside your usual life, and do these three things you ordinarily would not do:

1. <u>Dare to be vulnerable</u>: It's all right to admit you're human and capable of being hurt.

2. <u>Dare to disagree</u>: It's all right to voice opinions that are not popular.

3. <u>Dare to walk away</u>: It's all right to leave people who do not appreciate you or support you.

If you're alive, you know you're going to worry. The question is not whether you'll worry, but how you're going to *use* your worry to BENEFIT you. Worry can either make you sick, or make you act. It's your body, it's your life, it's your future. Decide now how you want to proceed. And PLEASE let me know!

Love,
Dr. Gilda

***

**Benefit from
Dr. Gilda's personal Advice & Coaching
www.DrGilda.com**

***

Dr. Gilda's Relationship Series
--8 Steps to a Sizzling Marriage
--8 Tips to Understand the Opposite Sex
--10 Questions Single Women Should Never Ask
& 10 They Should
--10 Signs of a Cheater-to-Be

Dr. Gilda's Self-Worth Series
--I'm Worth Loving! Here's Why.
--Ask for What You Want—AND GET IT!
--How to Be a Worry-Free Woman

Dr. Gilda's Fidelity Series
--Why Your Cheater Keeps Cheating—And You're Still There!
--How to Cope with the Cheater You Love—and WIN
--99 Prescriptions for Fidelity: *Your Rx for Trust*

ALSO
--Don't Bet on the Prince! *How to Have the Man You Want by Betting on Yourself*
--Don't Lie on Your Back for a Guy Who Doesn't Have Yours

***

Dr. Gilda Carle (Ph.D.) is an internationally known media personality and relationship expert. She has authored 15 books, including "Don't Bet on the Prince!" (a test question on "Jeopardy!"), "Teen Talk with Dr. Gilda," "He's Not All That!," "How to WIN When Your Mate Cheats" (winner of The London Book Festival literary award), "99 Prescriptions for Fidelity," and more. She also wrote the weekly "30-Second Therapist" column for the Today Show, and the "Ask Dr. Gilda" advice columnist for Match.com.

On TV, Dr. Gilda was the regular therapist for the Sally Jessy Raphael show, the "Love Doc" for MTV Online, and the TV host of "The Dr. Gilda Show" pilot for Twentieth Century Fox. In addition, she was the therapist in HBO's Emmy Award winner, "Telling Nicholas," featured on Oprah, where she guided a family to tell their 7-year-old that his mom died in the World Trade Center bombing.

In academia and the corporate sector, she has been a management consultant, Professor Emerita, motivational speaker, and product spokesperson.

As President of Country Cures, Inc., a non-profit

501(c)(3) educational charity organization, she is the "Country Music Doctor." As such, the organization uniquely uses country music to provide education and training for transitioning veterans and their families. If you, or someone you know, can benefit from this help, please see **www.CountryCures.org.**

Reach Dr. Gilda at
www.DrGilda.com
or
www.CountryCures.org

www.ingramcontent.com/pod-product-compliance
Lightning Source LLC
Chambersburg PA
CBHW071630040426
42452CB00009B/1569